Printed on acid-free paper.

ISBN 9780615226309

DEDICATIONS

For my mother
who believed in me,
supported me,
cared for me,
even while I was angry with her.

For my son, my Beloved,
Whose birth saved my life,
Whose Pure Love,
saved my soul.

CONTENTS

PREFACE

My Journey to Heart was a process that began long before the first entry into this book. It's a combination of blogs and poetry I wrote during my pregnancy and my son's first year outside of my womb. I chose to begin this culmination with my blog "Choice," simply because it felt right within my soul. It's also where the deepest realization the intensity of my true love occurred. I chose to keep the entries in the order I wrote them in my journals, rather than alter or categorize them. For me, the journey to heart has been a healing process that went from depression to pure joy, to elation, through the depths of hatred and rage, to sadness, anger, bitterness, which then led to a level of peace I believe, can only come from Pure Divine Surrender. It's been a beautiful ride and it is continuing on through the purest love that I've ever experienced. I thank you for reading this culmination of words that briefly explain the variety of emotions buried within during my healing process. It's truly been a beautiful journey and I enjoy sharing with you my process.

Peace and Blessings

"T"   September 2008

MY JOURNEY TO HEART

CHOICE

So I hold my head up high, smile and choose Me. God chose me to express as me in this lifetime, and express I will, fully with Love, Grace and Passion. Although a choice, I feel as if I have no choice, it was something put on me that I can no longer deny. Sometimes you have to walk away in order to fully choose the self. Choosing Me has been painful, but the most rewarding choice thus far.

My darling son, though you are a day late (so far) and I can't wait to hold you in my arms and kiss your little face, I can't say that I'm not glad that you are still my little secret. Well, my big bellied secret. I love you.

SIMPLICITY

Although always quite simple, pregnancy has taught me more about simplicity. It doesn't take a million poetic words to say, this is the most profoundly beautiful, yet challenging experience of my entire existence. I'm both excited and frightened.

Little boy I can't wait to see your face and hold you in my arms but sometimes I wish I could keep you inside of me all to myself, sharing you only with God. I do love you with a ferociousness that I've never felt.

Love
Mommy

RAGE

I tried to leave you. I saw who you were very early on and I tried to leave. Over and over I tried to leave, but you always managed to convince me to stay. Instead of listening to my instincts, I listened to you. All the lies, empty promises and words that had no action to back them up.

During the time I was most vulnerable and needed your care and protection, you inflicted on me the worst emotional abuse that I've ever experienced. Why, because I left you? I left you cause of the abuse. You fought and fought for a life you never wanted, at least not with me. Why didn't you just let me go? You were my biggest mistake that created my greatest Blessing. Now I have a precious gift from God to Love, Nurture and Raise to be a wonderful human being.

You wanna live your life, see women/have sex, whatever? That's your right. Well now that I'm moving on with mine, you yell at me, tell me I have nothing to offer, and tell me that if I get in a relationship or get married, that you're gonna cause "problems." What's that? Pure selfishness!

I AM ENRAGED and you aren't even worth it. Am I a victim? Only of my own choices!

FLASHBACK OF EMOTIONS

So as I'm driving today I'm thinking about the joys and beauty of breastfeeding. I'm smiling and then all of a sudden I remember the times my beautiful little boy was at my breast and his father was yelling at me. It was almost like a flashback of emotions so deeply intense, that I began to tear up while I was on my way to pick up my beloved from daycare. Breastfeeding is such a powerful, vulnerable time of bonding and nourishment. To have that interrupted by a man with a temper who would yell over the smallest of things, such as not getting his way, is such a profound violation.

I have so much awe and joy for all the women who had supportive men/partners in their life, who understood the power and importance of this time. Even if they weren't outwardly protective, they at least sat back and let a mother do what God, what Life gave to her to nourish and sustain the most awesome gift, a child.

Though his temper hasn't flared, towards me at least, for a little over a month, the wounds from his previous rageful outbursts still remain.

I prayed for forgiveness. I asked others to pray. Have I forgiven? I don't know anymore. I know to forgive has nothing to do with forgetting, but if I've forgiven, would the pain still be so strong?

EMOTIONAL ABUSE

Battered and bruised
beaten unrecognizable.
Only,
the wounds are unseen.
Why?
Your words were your weapon!

MOURNING

It's not about wanting you,
I haven't wanted you since before my pregnancy.
What it's about is the deep sadness I feel over a lost family.
I look at the friends I have in my life, whose husbands take them around with pride, their family.
And even when I do get married and have another child, my family will always be disrupted because of your mere existence.
I'm in mourning.
I would often say that my only mistake was in sleeping with you when I knew I didn't want to be with you.
Now I know there was a purpose. That purpose created a miracle, a pure gift from God.
As I look at him and watch him grow, I see all the Love, Joy and Peace that God intended for this world.
I stare with pure elation, an emotion only a mother would know.

NO!

The way you express your rage is not normal, it's not healthy, and it's NOT my fault. It was there before me and unless you get help it's gonna continue on being there after me.

BREASTFEEDING

Breastfeeding is my meditation.
It's the ultimate form of prayer.

I CAN'T TAKE IT

Your Misery is overwhelming.
I don't know what I did to you this time,
but I can't fuckin' take it anymore.
Your Happiness/Sadness is not my fault,
nor is it my problem.
I won't raise my son in an environment where he
will be made responsible for your happiness.
You've got a problem. FIX IT!

IS THERE?

Is there a place that exists, where sexual abuse is
not tolerated, dismissed, excused, covered up?
Is there a place here on earth where I can let my
child run free, yet be safe and protected?
Is there a place where I can raise him to be a good
man, a real man, the opposite of his father?
If there is I'll go there. Now! I'll pack up what I can
and leave. I'm the type of mother who raises her
son in freedom, with a dash of protectiveness,
plenty of trust, forgiveness, kindness, obedience,
sound judgment, and honesty. There's so much else
I want for him that I know I'm capable of giving,
holding the space for. I just need to get away from
this …
I think children deserve a certain amount of
freedom within a healthy cloud of protectiveness, in
a place where abuse of ANY kind is not tolerated,
excused or dismissed. My child deserves that and so
much more.

WHAT HAPPENS...

What happens when the only people you have to
turn to, are the very people you don't trust?
What happens when you know you're sane, but you
feel like you're going crazy?
I was led to apologize to those who used me.
Was that my fault, for believing?
Have Faith?
In what?
An unseen Force? Yes.
There is a Mighty Creator,
I believe.
Now why am I being fucked with?

WHAT A BLESSING!

What a Blessing it is to be a mother. Being a mother is very easy for me. Becoming a mother was the hardest thing I'd ever done. Loving on this level has been unreal and it just keeps on growing. I feel a sense Peace in who I am. I feel a sense of urgency to create the life I desire for my child. I thought my dreams were over, but they've only just begun. My whole world is opening up in ways I knew were possible, but began to believe were unreachable. I am so grateful, God I am so Grateful for this opportunity to Live, Love, Breathe, Be, to Mother.

FA

You were poison!
What you were was a toxic substance
that temporarily permeated my veins,
the veins of my consciousness.
You encouraged me to stay with abuse,
normalizing it based on your experiences.
Prognosis:
Clear!

CAN'T BELIEVE

I can't believe in "Like father, like son."
I birthed a part of you.
I guide that part, nurture him and though I'm in
surrender,
witnessing pure love and genius personified,
I secretly hope, pray,
that he comes out nothing like you.

NATURAL MOTHERING

There's a dance between mother and child that is
natural, NORMAL.
It needs the space to be; even to be cultivated if
necessary, definitely nurtured.
Society does what it does best,
mind other people's business. Maybe it's time for
society to get a life and mind its own fuckin'
business!

MOTHERING

Mothering is an intuitive ability that if nurtured and cultivated, can move mountains, can work wonders on the Human Race. Women need to be left alone to mother, not to be forced into a carbon copy of their mother or the expert du jour.

PONDERINGS

A Woman's emotions are her strength
medication denied me my emotions
ripped me of my clarity.
BUT,
it made me sane!

What is sanity anyway?
The absence of hysteria?
Levelheadedness?

MOTHER'S MILK

I feed you with my body
nourish you with my soul.
Mother's milk
Truly God's Gift

TRUE ARTISTIC ABILITY

To be a mother is to be an artist.
Think about it:
You've painted the perfect picture,
when you birthed your child.

HOW DO YOU MOURN A MOLESTER

By not going to the funeral!?.
I went to your grave today,
I stood over your dead body, buried 6 ft in the earth.
I said:
"I Fuckin' hate you for what you did to me!,"
to all the children you may have touched.
I would've spit on your grave, if I didn't have so
much love and respect for your mother.
I walked away
I mourned the person a few feet away.
I cried, told him I loved and missed him.
Walking back to my car,
forgiveness was screaming in my ear.
I walked back to your grave.
"I Forgive you" I said.
I Forgive you
for me.

WW

It's easy to be pure, easy going in life when you haven't been through societal scarification.
You may have had some bumps and bruises in life, but by birthright you haven't gone through generations of physical and emotional torture because of skin color and/or bloodlines.

LOST

I feel lost,
just a shadow of what I used to be,
dragging along in life not being seen or heard,
just stepped on.
I have so much to Live for.
So many Blessings.
The biggest of which,
Is my Beloved son.

I AM WORTHY!

I am worthy of vulnerability.
I deserve to feel safe within that space,
that vulnerability.
I deserve Life,
I'm worthy of feeling safe within that Life.
I deserve to be protected within the realm of safety
and vulnerability, and live out a fulfilled Life of my
desires.
My creativity
  attracts prosperity.
My Love
  attracts greater Love.
My reflection
  attracts healthy reflections.
My joyful words
  attracts healthy circumstances.
I am Healed, Healthy, Whole, Perfect and
Complete,
just as I am.
And you know what,
THAT'S OKAY!

I'M DONE

I spent my days walking on eggshells on top of a tightrope trying my best to create circumstances that would keep him from yelling at me, all the while trying to maintain my dignity and respect by not bending to his will. I then woke up and realized he was still in control whether he knew it or not. Why? Cause I was spending all my energy trying to walk a life that wouldn't piss him off, including downplaying my happiness and playing stupid. Just for some peace of mind.

Why?

Why do we tell our children strength comes from adversity? So they can glamorize hardships and make them a self-fulfilling prophecy?
Why can't we tell our children strength comes from within, and their reality can come from positive, healthy circumstances?

QUESTION

Can true forgiveness exist without a formal apology?

About the Author

T Christina is a work-at-home single mother who enjoys the purity of Being with Motherhood, while letting go of struggling in order to stay at home with her son.

www.ingramcontent.com/pod-product-compliance
Lightning Source LLC
Chambersburg PA
CBHW031336040426
42443CB00005B/367